AF585272

AUSTRALIA'S ENDANGERED ANIMALS ...AND THEIR HABITATS

A FOCUS ON ANTARCTIC TUNDRA

ICE AND SNOW HABITATS

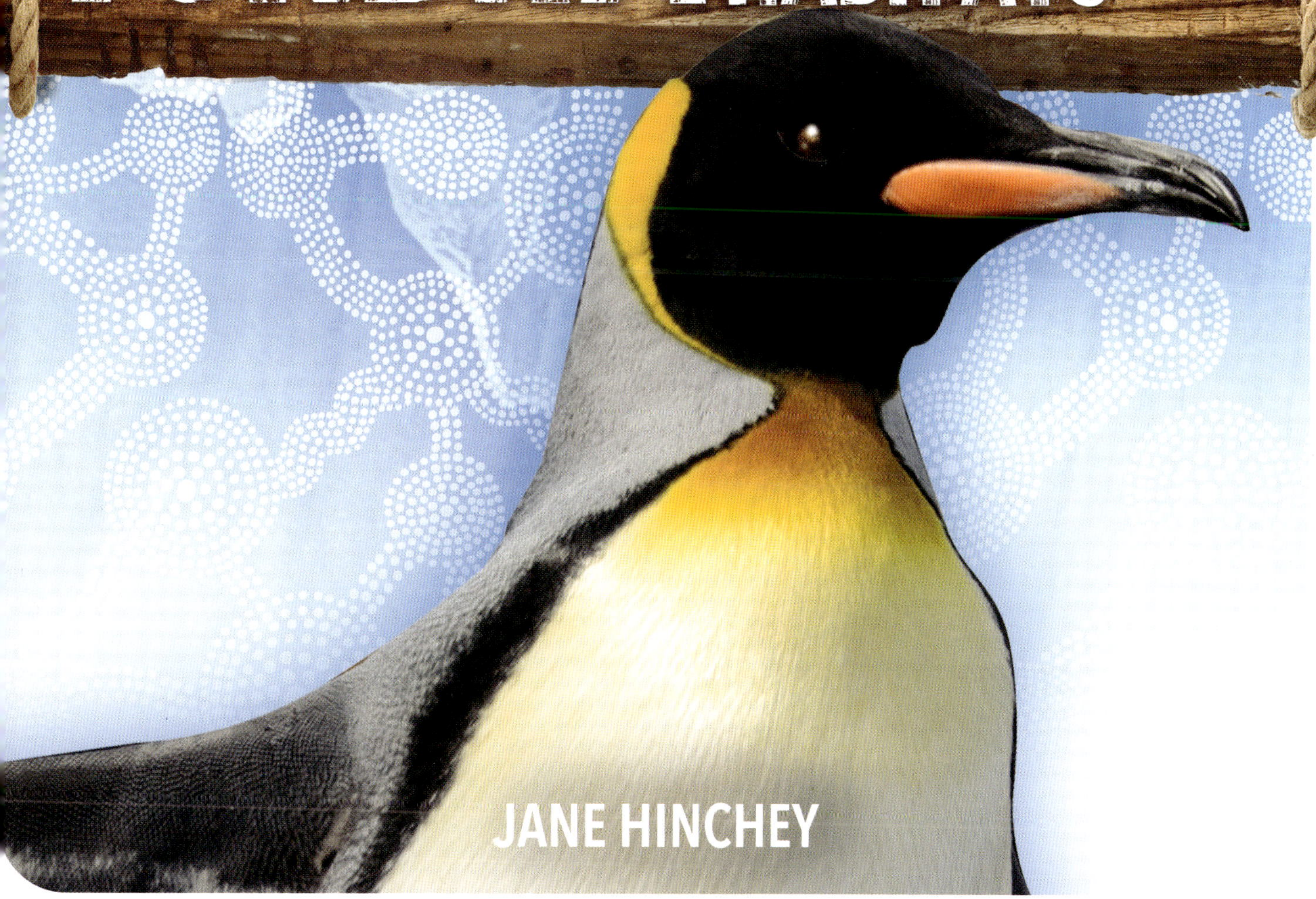

JANE HINCHEY

Redback Publishing
PO Box 357 Frenchs Forest NSW 2086
Australia

www.redbackpublishing.com.au
orders@redbackpublishing.com.au

ISBN 978-1-925630-73-2

Author: Jane Hinchey
Editor: Michael Anderson
Designer: Redback Publishing

Original illustrations © Redback Publishing 2019
Originated by Redback Publishing

Printed and bound in China

Acknowledgements
Abbreviations: l–left, r–right, b–bottom, t–top, c–centre, m–middle
We would like to thank the following for permission to reproduce photographs: (Images © shutterstock)
p5 By I, Beentree (Kookaburra Eggs), p6br By Photo by Phil Spark, p13tl By NASA Goddard Space Flight Center from Greenbelt, MD, USA, p15mr By Gregg Yan, p17t CherylRamalho, p22bl By NASA Goddard Space Flight Center from Greenbelt, MD, USA, p23tl By JJ Harrison, p30t By Photo by Phil Spark.

Every effort has been made to contact copyright holders of any material reproduced in this book. Any omissions will be rectified in subsequent printings if notice is given to the publisher.

NATIONAL LIBRARY OF AUSTRALIA

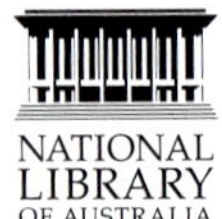

A catalogue record for this book is available from the National Library of Australia

CONTENTS

Antarctica is the coldest, driest and windiest continent on Earth. 98 per cent of the continent is covered by ice with no tundra, trees or bushes. There are also permanently ice-free areas that cover about 1 per cent of the continent. This is the subantarctic region, immediately north of the Antarctic region. Antarctica does not have its own government, nor does it belong to one country, although there are numerous pending historical claims. Governance is carried out by 29 consultative nations at an annual Antarctic Treaty Consultative Meeting. Each of the consultative nations has one or more base on the continent. Each Antarctic base is governed by the national laws of its home country.

Antarctic Treaty

July 1957 to December 1958 was known as International Geophysical Year. At this time there were 12 countries active in Antarctica. These countries were Argentina, Australia, Belgium, Chile, France, Japan, New Zealand, Norway, South Africa, the U.S.S.R., the United Kingdom and the United States of America. These countries were invited by the USA to a conference where a treaty to ensure in the interests of all mankind that Antarctica shall continue forever to be used exclusively for peaceful purposes and shall not become the scene or object of international discord.

These original 12 nations were later joined by Brazil, Bulgaria, the People's Republic of China, Ecuador, Finland, Germany, India, Italy, South Korea, Netherlands, Peru, Poland, Spain, Sweden and Uruguay to form the Consultative Parties. There are also 24 Non-Consultative Parties who are signatories to the treaty.

The treaty is a short document focussing on peace, cooperation, non-nuclearisation, free exchange of scientific results, territorial sovereignty, preventing new claims and setting aside arguments over the existing ones.

The Antarctic Treaty came into effect in 1961, dedicating the continent to peaceful scientific investigation. All territorial claims were suspended. 53 countries have now signed the treaty, which has resulted in Antarctica being a peaceful place, never affected by war.

AUSTRALIA ANIMAL CLASSIFICATION CHART

Scientists classify animals into groups in order to study and understand them. Each group can have numerous sub-groups. Australia's animals are divided into six major groups.

AMPHIBIAN	Lives on both land and water Has smooth skin, webbed feet Lays eggs	Frogs such as the spotted tree frog and corroboree frog
BIRD	Hatches from eggs Has feathers and wings	Australian bustard, cassowary, kookaburra
FISH	Lives in water Hatch from soft eggs Has fins and scales	Fish such as the Eastern freshwater cod, Australian smelt and estuary perch
MAMMAL	Warm blooded Lactate to feed young Most have body hair	Koala, wombat, kangaroo, wallaby, possum
REPTILE	Hatches from eggs Lives on land Has scales	Eastern bearded dragon, eastern brown snake, freshwater crocodile
INVERTEBRATES	No backbone Many forms of locomotion	Beetles, flies, mosquitoes, snails, worms, crabs, squid and spiders such as the redback spider

CLASSIFICATION AND IDENTIFICATION

Australia has the worst mammal extinction rate in the world. Globally, one out of three mammal extinctions in the last 400 years has occurred in Australia. Furthermore, over 1,700 plant and animal species are listed as threatened with extinction.

There are thousands of fauna species living in Australia's different habitats, with new species being discovered every year. The use of an international classification system is extremely important.

When identifying characteristics that make a species vulnerable, the international classification system used is overseen by the International Union for the Conservation of Nature (IUCN) red list.

Species in the Critically Endangered, Endangered and Vulnerable categories are all considered 'threatened.'

The International Union for Conservation of Nature

Many factors are used to assess the conservation status of a species. The International Union for Conservation of Nature is the global authority on the status of the natural world and the actions needed to protect it. The IUCN gathers data about different species from a huge range of sources, such as biologists, conservationists and statisticians.

The IUCN Red List of Threatened Species is recognised globally as the authority on the status of endangered animals. It divides species into nine different categories:

- Extinct (EX)
- Extinct in the Wild (EW)
- Critically Endangered (CR)
- Endangered (EN)
- Vulnerable (VU)
- Near Threatened (NT)
- Least Concern (LC)
- Data Deficient (DD)
- Not Evaluated (NE)

Classification for the MOUNTAIN PYGMY POSSUM

Species:parvus
Genus:Burramys
Family:Burramyidae
Order:Diprotodontia
Subclass:Marsupialia
Class:Mammalia
Subphylum:Vertebrata
Phylum:Chordata
Kingdom:Animalia

EXTINCT ANIMALS

In Australia, animals are classified at both State and Federal levels. At Federal level the current categories are:

- Extinct
- Extinct in the Wild
- Critically Endangered
- Endangered
- Vulnerable
- Conservation Dependent

Extinction is when every single member of a species dies and none are left alive.

Scientists go to great lengths to determine that a species is extinct – a process that begins with careful monitoring of the species while it still exists.

Since European settlement, 24 birds, 7 frogs and 27 mammal species or subspecies have become extinct in Australia.

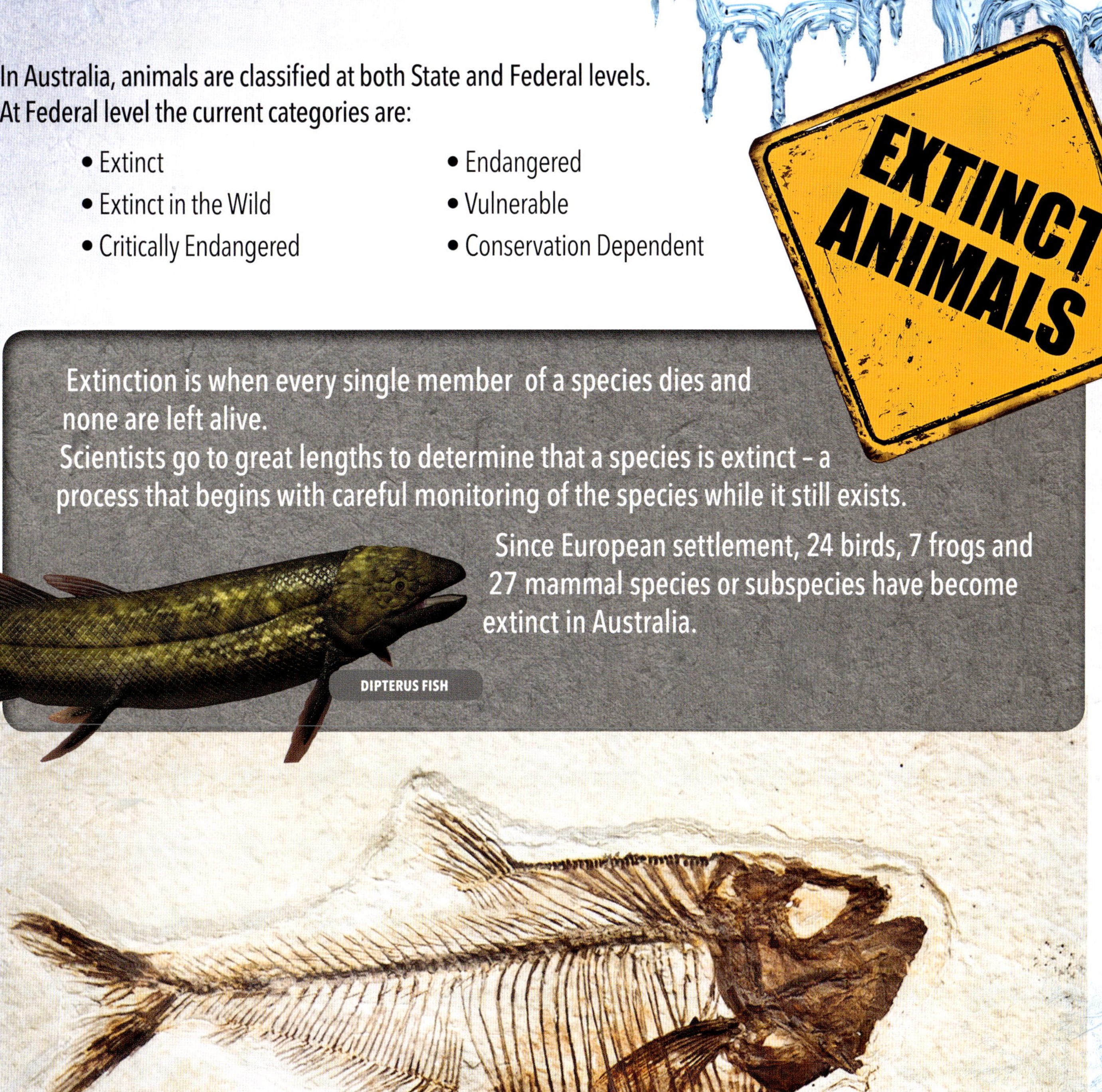

DIPTERUS FISH

Classification

There are many ways to classify species. We can choose any characteristic as a basis for sorting animals. These may include body form, colour pattern, mode of development or genetics. Classification helps organise the differences within and between groups of animals. Classification of animals helps identify them, understand them, quantify the threat to them and take steps to conserve a species.

AUSTRALIAN ANTARCTIC TERRITORY

Australia is unique. It is not only a country and an island, but also one of the world's seven continents. Australia was cut off from the rest of the world's landmass for over 100 million years, which allowed for a diverse range of animals to flourish. It is home to more than one million species of plants and animals, many of which are found nowhere else in the world, and less than half have been described scientifically. About 85 per cent of plants, 84 per cent of mammals, 45 per cent of birds, 88 per cent of reptiles and 94 per cent of amphibians are endemic. In Australia there are more than 378 species of mammals, 828 species of birds, 300 species of lizards, 140 species of snakes and two species of crocodiles.

Tundra, Ice and Snow

Not all of Australia is beaches or desert. Australia has a diverse array of environments and ecosystems, including snow covered mountains and barren islands in the Antarctic.

FAST FACT

Only four countries recognize Australia's claim to sovereignty in Antarctica:

- New Zealand
- France
- Norway
- United Kingdom

How is Antarctica a Part of Australia?

Antarctica is Earth's only continent without a native human population. The majority of Antarctica is claimed by one or more countries, although these claims are not officially recognised. In 1961 the Antarctic Treaty came into force between 12 countries: Argentina, Australia, Belgium, Chile, France, Japan, New Zealand, Norway, South Africa, the Soviet Union, the United Kingdom and the USA. Between them, these countries had already established over 50 Antarctic stations, so the treaty was a formalisation of the cooperation that had been achieved between these countries operational and scientific communities. The treaty now has 53 parties.

Australian Antarctic Territory (AAT) is a part of Antarctica that is administered by Australia. Overseeing it is the Australian Antarctic Division, which is an agency of the federal government's Department of the Environment and Energy.

The Australian Antarctic Territory covers nearly 5.9 million square kilometres, about 42 per cent of Antarctica and the subantarctic islands of Macquarie, Heard and McDonald. The population is less than 1,000.

The Australian Antarctic Division maintains four permanent research stations occupied year round by scientists and support staff.

- Mawson, Davis and Casey are on the Antarctic continent.
- Macquarie Island is in the subantarctic.

The Division also manages Heard and McDonald Islands, Commonwealth Bay and keeps a weather station at Dome A, the highest point in Antarctica.

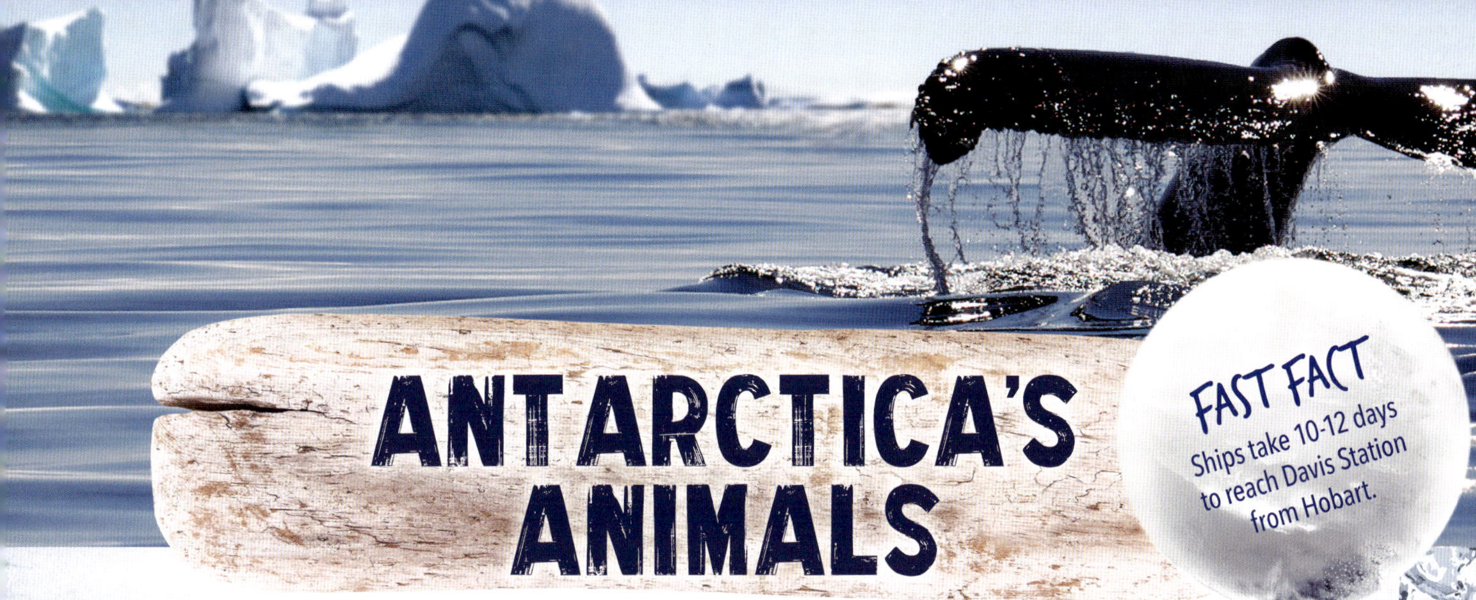

ANTARCTICA'S ANIMALS

FAST FACT
Ships take 10-12 days to reach Davis Station from Hobart.

You will not see native Australian animals such as the kangaroo or koala on Antarctica, however, Antarctica is home to a wide range of penguins, whales, seals, krill, land invertebrates and seabirds such as albatross and terns.

Antarctica's Animals

Australia takes conservation of Antarctica's flora and fauna and the preservation of the natural environment seriously. In 1991, the parties of the Antarctic Treaty came together to sign the Madrid Protocol, which is the framework for protecting the Antarctic environment. This designates Antarctica as a natural reserve, devoted to peace and science and requires that care for the environment is a fundamental consideration in all activities.

The Committee for Environmental Protection (CEP) was established under the Madrid Protocol, comprising of members from all 35 countries that are party to the protocol. The CEP currently:

- prevents the introduction of non-native species to Antarctica
- manages the environmental implications of climate change
- addresses how Antarctic tourism interacts with the environment
- addresses environmental challenges from activities conducted before the Madrid Protocol entered into force. These include the clean-up of past waste disposal sites and abandoned facilities
- the development of Antarctic protected areas

SNAPSHOT

Official name: The Australian Antarctic Territory (AAT)
Government: Australian external territory
Total area: 5.9 million square kilometres
Capital: Davis Station
Currency: Australian dollar

Population: less than 1,000
Largest research station: Mirny Station (Russia)
Sovereign state: Australia
Chief scientist: Gwen Fenton
Highest point: Mawson Peak at 2,745 metres

TUNDRA, ICE AND SNOW HABITATS

A habitat is a place that provides shelter, safety, food and water for the animals that live there. The creatures and plants all do things to help keep the whole habitat healthy and in balance and rely upon each other for their survival. Animals like cockroaches eat the dead plants and recycle the nutrients back into the soil, which helps the other plants to grow. Bats, birds and insects help spread seeds. Every plant and creature serves a purpose.

Australia is a large country with many different climates that has contributed to its range of habitats. These habitats extend from Antarctica to the tropics, encompassing environments as diverse as oceans and coasts, mangroves and rivers, coastal heathlands, mountain forests and rainforests, alpine meadows, woodlands and the dry grasslands of the interior. Each habitat can also include smaller habitats within it. For example, in the harsh subantarctic environment there may be a vegetation-covered shelter within a barren rocky outcrop.

Tundra, ice and snow habitats range from the alpine mountains and forests of the Snowy Mountains, to Australian Antarctic Territory.

What is Tundra?

Tundra is a treeless polar desert, found where the tree growth is hindered by low temperatures. Tundra generally has large stretches of bare rocks and earth, with patchy low vegetation such as mosses, lichens, herbs and small shrubs.

There are three types of tundra:

- Arctic tundra
- Antarctic tundra
- Alpine tundra

Australia's tundra regions such as the subantarctic islands - Macquarie, Heard and McDonald.

Subantarctic and Antarctic

Antarctica is the coldest, driest and windiest continent on Earth. About 98 per cent of the continent is covered by ice with no tundra, trees or bushes. When you think of Antarctica, you probably picture ice and glaciers and you would be mainly right. Yet most Antarctic animals live in the permanently ice-free areas that cover about 1 per cent of the continent. This is the subantarctic region, immediately north of the Antarctic region.

Alpine Areas

Compared to many other countries, Australia does not have very tall mountains so only has a small alpine area. The Alps support many different flora and fauna communities at altitudes above 300 to 2,228 metres above sea level. In total, the land above the tree line, above 1,850 metres, is less than 80 square kilometres. Snow lies on Australia's highest mountains for about 120 days each year.

Alpine areas encompass a range of habitats, including:

- Grasslands
- Heathlands
- Bogs and swamp areas
- Rocky slopes and boulders

HEATHLANDS

Tall alpine heathlands and herbfields dominate the high alpine landscape. About 200 species of plants, such as prickly snow grass and alpine wallaby grass, are found in the alpine areas. Sphagnum sedges and heath grow at alpine bogs and alpine marsh marigold grows in areas below the snowdrift. A high percentage of alpine species are endemic.

WHAT DO ANTARCTIC HABITATS LOOK LIKE?

Pack Ice

Huge floating pieces of sea ice, called pack ice, form during the winter, more than doubling the size of the Antarctic continent. Pack ice melts in the spring and summer. It is not attached to a shoreline and is moved by the wind and ocean currents. Weddell seals, the most southerly dwelling of all mammals, live at the edge of pack ice. They use cracks and holes in the ice to breath. Climate change affects pack ice and the animals that live and feed around it.

Antarctic Waters

The ocean is home to whales, seals and fish. Birds such as penguins and albatross all live in or rely on these waters. Antarctic ice fish have an antifreeze protein that keeps their blood flowing.

Vast Ice-covered Land

Vast areas of Antarctica, including mountains, are covered by an ice sheet that is up to four kilometres thick. This ice covers 98 per cent of Antarctica. Despite the harshness of this landscape, there are different species of penguins, seals and birds to be found here.

FAST FACT

15 species of flying birds, including the endangered Southern Giant Petrel, use Heard Island as a breeding ground.

Islands with Glaciers

In the subantarctic region there are many small islands. Heard Island is covered in glaciers. A number of seal species live on Heard Island, such as the leopard seal, subantarctic fur seal, Antarctic fur seal and the southern elephant seal.

Ice-free Islands

Macquarie Island is ice-free, with no permanent snow cover. It is an important region for seals and seabirds that breed there.

Rocky Islets

Rocky areas, such as the McDonald islands are natural habitats for birds and seals and a number of endemic invertebrates.

ENDANGERED, THREATENED AND VULNERABLE

ENDANGERED SPECIES AREA

Not all the animals mentioned in this book are listed as Endangered, however many are still Vulnerable or Near Threatened. Some species are listed as Least Concern, but their numbers are decreasing. Others may be stable, but their habitats are under threat. The habitats of the Antarctic region are at risk from global warming, increased fishing and tourism, marine pollution and invasive species. These areas support a diverse array of creatures and they are impacted by any changing environmental conditions.

ADAPTING TO THE COLD

Antarctic animals survive in freezing conditions by reducing the body heat that is lost. This can be through behaviours, such as huddling together like the emperor penguins, or by physical means evolved over time. Some of these physical adaptations include:

- Thick waterproof and windproof coats: Many Antarctic animals such as emperor penguins have coats that protect them from freezing water and wind.
- Thick layer of fat: Whales, seals and some penguin have layers of blubber that insulate them from the freezing conditions. Male elephant seals can use their blubber as an energy reserve and live off their fat reserves during summer.
- Extremities such as bills and flippers are smaller, meaning less blood is needed for these areas and therefore less heat is lost.

FAST FACT

Around 88 per cent of species in the Southern Ocean are found nowhere else in the world.

Research Projects

Research projects in the Australian Antarctic Territory (AAT) record the status and trends of wildlife populations that are of ecological or conservation value. Long-term research projects include:

- Assessing change in krill distribution.
- The impact of climate change.
- Changes to seabird populations.
- Antarctic baleen whale habitats.
- Population and distribution of the endangered Antarctic blue whale.
- Macquarie Island albatrosses and giant petrels.

Research projects help inform conservation and management options for Antarctica's wildlife and assist in according animals the correct conservation status on *Australia's Environment Protection and Biodiversity Conservation Act 1999 (EPBC Act)* and the IUCN Red List of Threatened Species (IUCN Red List).

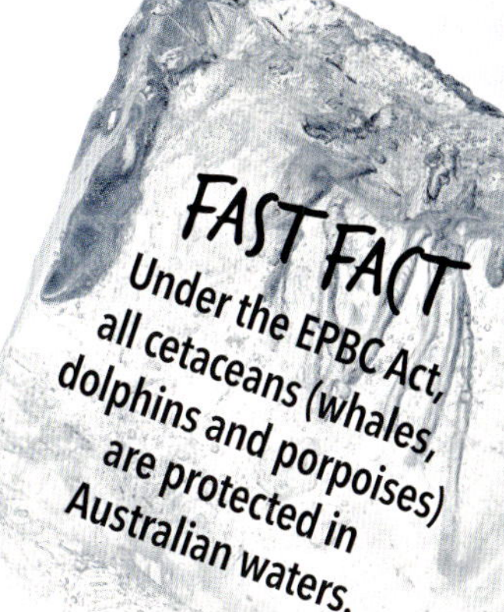

ANIMALS UNDER THREAT

Southern Right Whale	Amsterdam Albatross	Chatham Albatross
Sei Whale	Antipodean Albatross	Campbell Albatross
Blue Whale	Tristan Albatross	Salvin's Albatross
Fin Whale	Southern Royal Albatross	White-capped Albatross
Humpback Whale	Wandering Albatross	White-bellied Storm Petrel
Magellanic Penguin	Northern Royal Albatross	Antarctic Tern
Emperor Penguin	Sooty Albatross	Southern Elephant Seal
King Penguin	Buller's Albatross	Soft-plumaged Petrel
Rockhopper Penguin	Indian Yellow-nosed Albatross	Kermadec Petrel
Macaroni Penguin	Shy Albatross	Abbott's Booby
Adelie Penguin	Grey-headed Albatross	
Gentoo Penguin		

ABBOTT'S BOOBY

HUMPBACK WHALE

BLUE WHALE

WHAT IS THE PROBLEM?

Why are so many of Australia's species under threat?
There are a number of major issues impacting native animals.

Climate Change

Climate change is the greatest threat to Antarctica. Global warming and a rise in sea temperatures will impact land and sea ice. Already, some huge shelves of ice have collapsed and glaciers have diminished in size. This will affect Antarctic and subantarctic habitats in numerous ways including directly altered weather patterns and rising sea levels. These events could disrupt the normal cycle of variability to which animals and plants have adapted. Increased emissions of CO2 to the atmosphere are partly absorbed by oceans, which increases the acidity of ocean waters and changes the physiology of marine organisms. Rising sea temperatures will also affect microscopic plankton, resulting in changes to the whole ocean eco-system.

Research shows that ice-free areas in Antarctica could expand by close to 25 per cent by 2100. This would drastically change the animal and plant life of the continent.

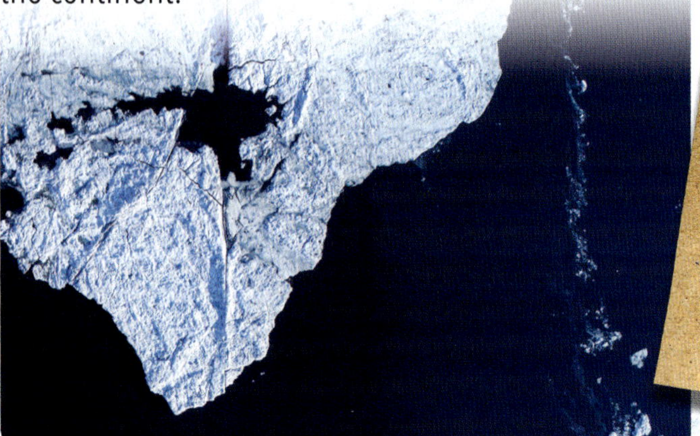

Changing Ecosystems

An animal's survival often depends on the animal's ecosystem maintaining balance. Any change to the ecosystem can impact the species living there. One example of this is the food chain. The loss of the smallest creature can affect the larger creatures that feed off them, all the way to the top of the food chain. These interconnected food webs are an essential part of the overall ecosystem. Even the smallest change in an ecosystem can have a major impact.

DID YOU KNOW?

Rising sea levels won't only impact marine animals. Many other animals will be impacted. One study predicts that 14 per cent of Northern NSW's koala habitats will experience saltwater inundation over the next 50 years. This would increase toxins in gum trees and reduce the koala's food availability.

Human Interference

People have been visiting Antarctica for over 100 years. Although there are now treaties in place that provide strict guidelines on what activities can take place there and how to treat the environment, this was not always the case. Hunting for seals and whales and fishing began in the 18th century. Early exploration teams left their mark on the formerly pristine environment. After the signing of the Antarctic Treaty, countries were responsible for cleaning up human waste, however each country did this in different ways. Some countries removed the waste from the continent, whilst others simply buried it.

Under the Madrid Protocol, waste produced at research camps now must be disposed of in ice pits or shipped back to Australia. In recent years, waste from the past has also been shipped back.

Overfishing

Large scale fishing began in the 1970s. Many species were hunted or fished to near extinction. Birds like albatross and petrels were entangled in fishing lines and nets. Overfishing of krill, a fish essential to the overall food web, peaked at 500,000 tonnes in the early 1980s.

While the Southern Ocean experiences less fishing than other oceans, due to expense and dangerous sea conditions, it is still overfished. In 1980, the Commission on the Conservation of the Antarctic Marine Living Resources began and the members started meeting annually to discuss the conservation of marine species in the area. The Convention does not prohibit fishing, but it does focus on managing the fisheries. Nowadays, fishing boats must have a license, which sets a specific area and period to fish as well as the species and catch that is allowed. Boats must contain satellite-monitoring devices that can communicate their location. Failure to do so can result in the revoking of the license.

Tourism to Antarctica is rising rapidly. To reduce the impact of this growing trend, annual numbers are capped. In 2016-2017, there were 44,202 visitors. A visitor could unknowingly bring in foreign seeds or spores that introduce an alien species to this pristine environment. Therefore all care is taken to manage tourism.

MARINE MESS

Marine animals often mistake plastic for jellyfish and eat it, or they become entangled in it.

Strangling the Ocean

Most litter takes hundreds of years to break down, during which time it continues to pollute the ocean and damage marine life. Items such as plastic bags and rings from plastic 'six-packs' can entangle or get eaten by animals, including fish, marine birds, dolphins, whales and seals.

Up to 12.7 million tonnes of plastic waste is washed into the world's ocean each year. There are now more than 46,000 pieces of plastic floating in every 2.5 square kilometres of the ocean. These plastics are wreaking havoc with marine animals. Ocean currents can shift dangerous pollution hundreds of kilometres from its original source. Plastic debris kills more than 1 million seabirds every year, as well as more than 100,000 marine mammals.

For a long time scientists thought that Antarctica remained plastic free, however recent research shows that, like the rest of the world's oceans, the Southern Ocean is also contaminated by plastics. In fact, the problem there is far worse than ever imagined.

Microplastics

A major environmental concern is the use of microplastics, or microbeads. Many modern cosmetics and household products contain tiny particles of plastic that have a devastating impact on marine life.

These products include:

- facial scrub
- body scrub
- toothpaste
- deodorant
- lipstick
- eyeliner
- washing detergent
- cleaning products

Other plastic products such as water and soda bottles or plastic bags can also break down into miniscule particles creating pieces of microplastic. This impacts the wildlife in the area, specifically the krill, which are the foundation of the food chain. Krill then pass harmful chemicals on to all the animals that consume them.

Scientists have estimated that approximately 500 kilograms of microplastics from personal care products and nearly 30 billion clothing fibres make their way into the Southern Ocean each decade. With more research activities, fishing and tourism in the region, this will rise.

FAST FACT

The United States banned the use of microbeads in 2017, but Australia is still relying on individual companies to phase these destructive products out themselves.

DISRUPTING THE FOOD CHAIN

When one species is threatened, the complex habitat and food web it is a part of also becomes threatened. A food chain is a sequence of which animals eat what, while the food web links all the food chains together. The food chain from the Antarctic region encompasses many species from marine algae and tiny plankton to large sharks, whales and dugong. While a larger species might not eat krill directly, it could feed on the creatures that do. When one link in the food chain or web is threatened, it puts the entire ecosystem in danger.

THE IMPORTANCE OF KRILL

The Antarctic ecosystem relies on krill. This tiny shrimp-like organism is the key prey species for many creatures, including fish, seal, seabirds and whales. Blue whales can eat 4 tonne a day while baleen whales can consume thousands of tonne. Countless species are dependent on krill, which means that if the krill population is compromised, all other species would be impacted.

THE TERRITORY OF HEARD ISLAND AND MCDONALD ISLANDS

Heard and McDonald Islands are Australian external territories located in the Southern Ocean, closer to Antarctica than to Australia. The islands have been an Australian territory since 1947. Although unknown to most Australians, the Islands are Australia's only sovereign Territory in the Southern Indian Ocean sector of the globe.

The islands are barren and volcanic. There are no ports or harbours and the islands are surrounded by dangerous waters, so are difficult to reach and inhospitable for humans. There has been very little human interference on the islands so they remain in pristine condition, with undamaged ecosystems and no introduced plant or animal species. The flora and fauna of Heard and McDonald Islands have evolved naturally. Because of this, these unique islands received a World Heritage Listing in 1997.

LEOPARD SEAL

Some of the animals that live on and around the Islands:

- sperm whale
- fin whale
- leopard seal
- subantarctic fur seal
- Antarctic fur seal
- southern elephant seal
- subantarctic land snail
- lantern fish
- icefish
- moray cod
- marbled cod
- some species of mites, beetles, moths, weevils, fleas and flies

ICEFISH

SPERM WHALE

SUBANTARCTIC FUR SEAL

FIN WHALE

FAST FACT

Australia's only two active volcanoes are found in The Territory of Heard and McDonald Islands.

Human Involvement on the Islands

No one lives on these islands. Since the first landing on Heard Island in 1855, human activity in the area has been limited. There have been approximately 240 landings on Heard Island and only two landings on McDonald Island, in 1971 and 1980. Early landings on Heard Island were due to sealing in the area, but more recently, visits have been for research and scientific purposes.

Shore parties consist of scientists and some support crew who set up camps for anything from a few weeks to a few months. The Australian Antarctic Division has also performed environmental management activities, such as removing waste material from Atlas Cove. Most waste is shipped to Australia to be dealt with.

There have been a number of private landings on Heard Island, however numbers remain small despite the growth in visits to other subantarctic and Antarctic sites.

Research in the area focuses on climate change and the impact on the biodiversity and ecosystems of Heard Island. Research disciplines include:

- Geology
- Vulcanology
- Ecology
- Glaciology
- Geomorphology
- Meteorology
- Terrestrial and marine ecology
- Oceanography
- Cultural and heritage study

HEARD ISLAND

The largest of the group of islands, Heard Island is mountainous, dominated by Big Ben, an active volcano that at 2,475 metres high dwarfs any mountain on mainland Australia.

The island is 80 per cent covered by ice, including 41 glaciers. Microfossil records show that ferns and woody plants were once present on the island, around 65 million to 2.58 million years ago, however they do not exist there today. Heard Island has the smallest number of plant species of any of the subantarctic island groups, which reveals just how isolated it is. Flora includes low-growing herbaceous flowering plants and vegetation and numerous moss and algae species.

Heard Island is a breeding ground for 15 species of flying birds, including the endangered Southern Giant Petrel.

McDonald Islands

HEARD ISLAND SHAG

Conservation Status: Vulnerable under *Australia's Environment Protection and Biodiversity Conservation Act 1999.*

The Heard Island shag is black with white underparts. It has white around the head and white bars on its wings. They are social creatures, roosting in groups of up to several hundred birds. They breed from late August to early October, with the eggs laid a couple of months later. They feed on marine worms and small fish.

One potential threat to the Heard Island shag is climate change, which affects sea temperatures and therefore the shag's food web.

Whilst found on both Heard Island and McDonald Island, it only breeds on Heard Island. Because of its extremely localised habitat and breeding ground, any changes to habitat, including weather conditions and food availability will affect the shag's survival. The Heard Island Shag is listed as Vulnerable.

MCDONALD ISLANDS

Located 44 kilometres to the west of Heard Island, the McDonald Islands are small, totalling about 2.5 square kilometres. The main island has a sloping plateau on the northern side while the south side is a steep hill. The smaller islands are rocky islets.

The volcano on McDonald Island was dormant for 75,000 years. It has erupted several times since 1992.

A survey of the island in 1980 showed that the McDonald Island's plant life was less diverse than that of Heard Island. Four mosses and a number of algae species were recorded, along with some fungi.

On McDonald Island, 23 species of marine mammals are found, including seals, whales, dolphins and a porpoise. There are 11 species of birds that are similar to the birds on Heard Island.

OCEAN GIANTS

Whales

Threats to whale populations include climate change, underwater noise pollution, fishing nets, widespread plastic pollution and ship strikes. Whales have a very slow reproductive rate with adult females giving birth to one calf every few years. Australian waters are an important habitat for many species of whales. Five whale species are listed under Australia's Environment Protection and Biodiversity Conservation Act (EPBC) as nationally threatened, and all are found in the Southern Ocean.

- blue whale (endangered)
- southern right whale (endangered)
- sei whale (vulnerable)
- fin whale (vulnerable)
- humpback whale (vulnerable)

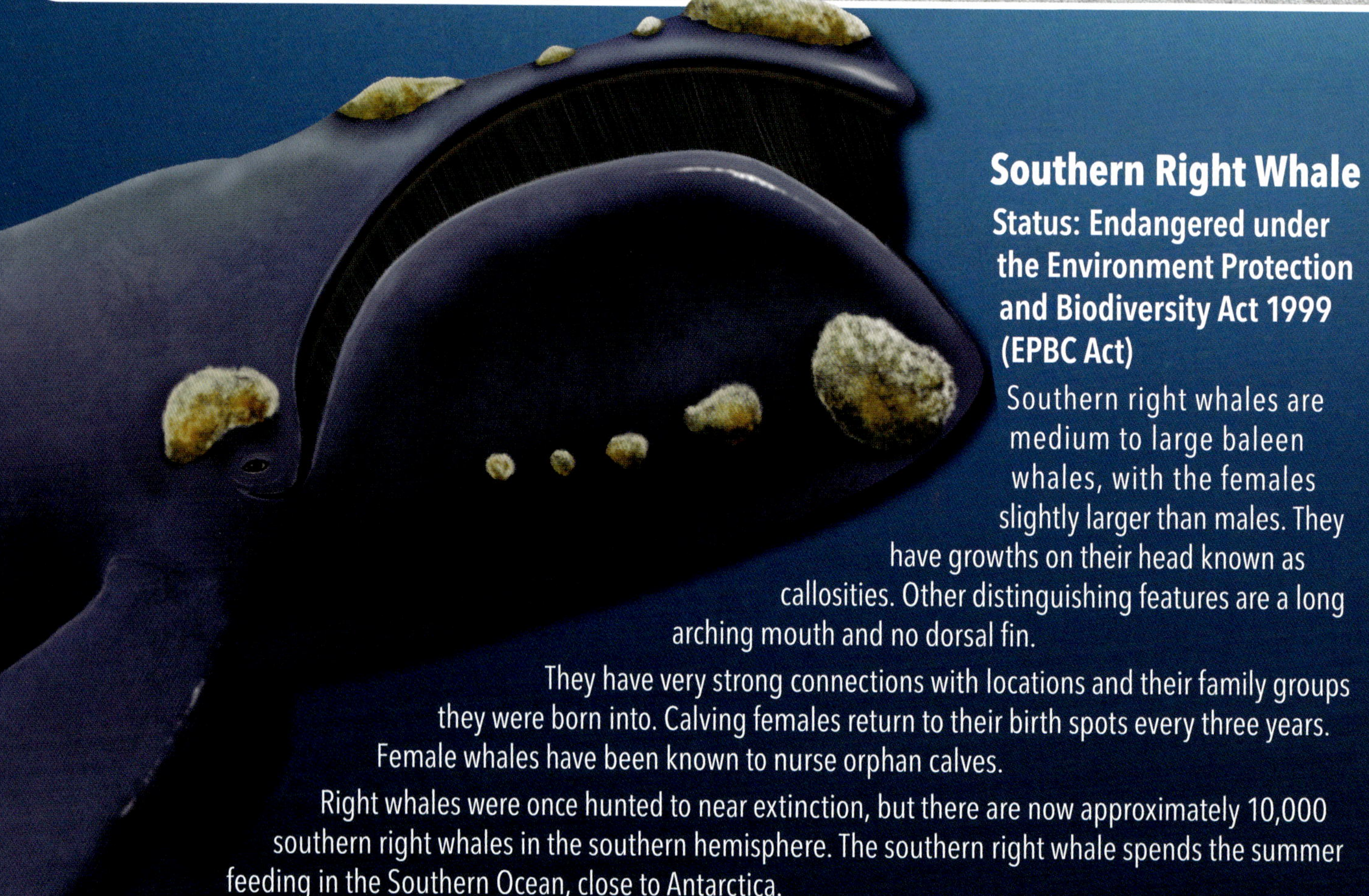

Southern Right Whale

Status: Endangered under the Environment Protection and Biodiversity Act 1999 (EPBC Act)

Southern right whales are medium to large baleen whales, with the females slightly larger than males. They have growths on their head known as callosities. Other distinguishing features are a long arching mouth and no dorsal fin.

They have very strong connections with locations and their family groups they were born into. Calving females return to their birth spots every three years. Female whales have been known to nurse orphan calves.

Right whales were once hunted to near extinction, but there are now approximately 10,000 southern right whales in the southern hemisphere. The southern right whale spends the summer feeding in the Southern Ocean, close to Antarctica.

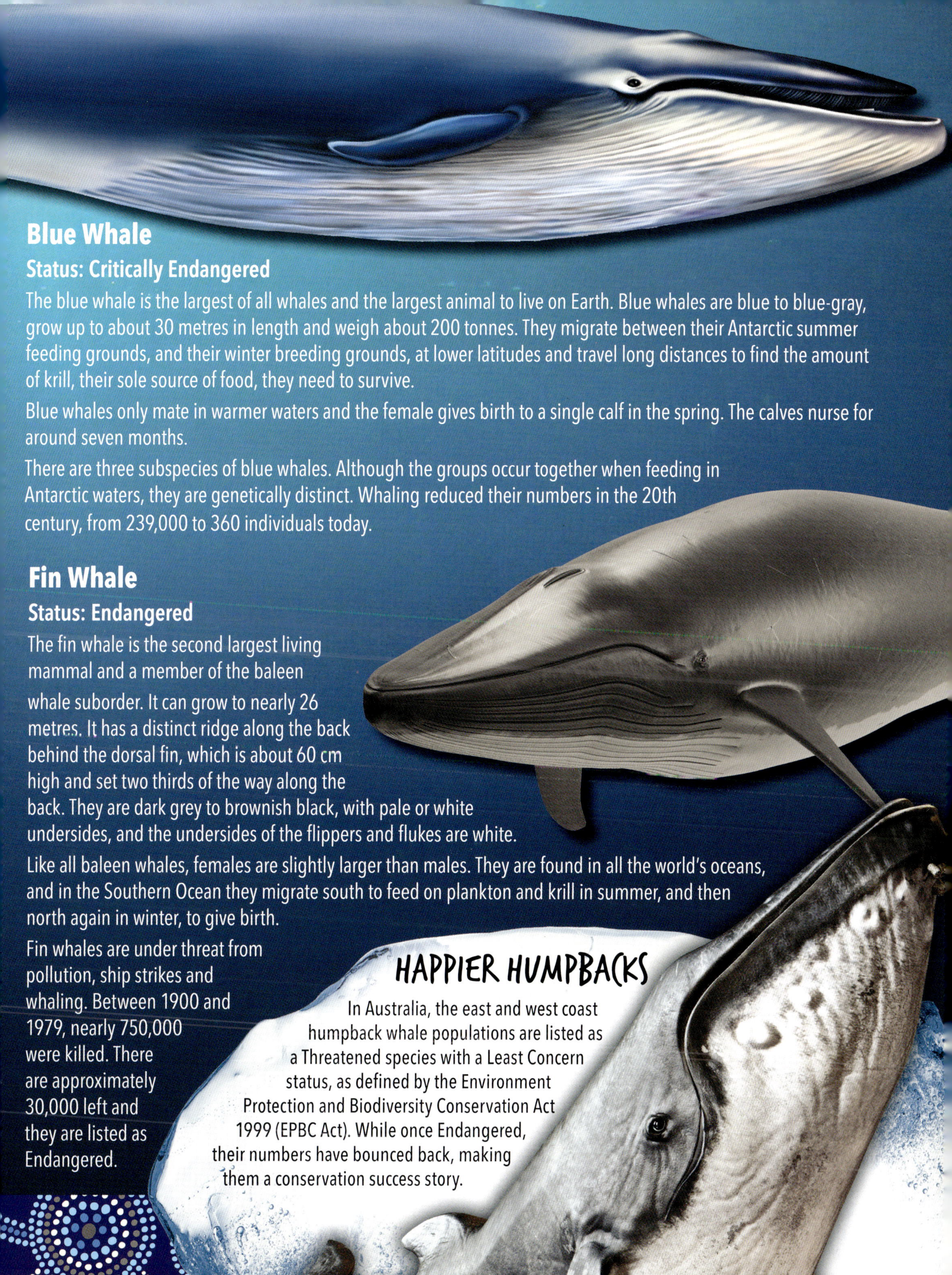

Blue Whale

Status: Critically Endangered

The blue whale is the largest of all whales and the largest animal to live on Earth. Blue whales are blue to blue-gray, grow up to about 30 metres in length and weigh about 200 tonnes. They migrate between their Antarctic summer feeding grounds, and their winter breeding grounds, at lower latitudes and travel long distances to find the amount of krill, their sole source of food, they need to survive.

Blue whales only mate in warmer waters and the female gives birth to a single calf in the spring. The calves nurse for around seven months.

There are three subspecies of blue whales. Although the groups occur together when feeding in Antarctic waters, they are genetically distinct. Whaling reduced their numbers in the 20th century, from 239,000 to 360 individuals today.

Fin Whale

Status: Endangered

The fin whale is the second largest living mammal and a member of the baleen whale suborder. It can grow to nearly 26 metres. It has a distinct ridge along the back behind the dorsal fin, which is about 60 cm high and set two thirds of the way along the back. They are dark grey to brownish black, with pale or white undersides, and the undersides of the flippers and flukes are white.

Like all baleen whales, females are slightly larger than males. They are found in all the world's oceans, and in the Southern Ocean they migrate south to feed on plankton and krill in summer, and then north again in winter, to give birth.

Fin whales are under threat from pollution, ship strikes and whaling. Between 1900 and 1979, nearly 750,000 were killed. There are approximately 30,000 left and they are listed as Endangered.

HAPPIER HUMPBACKS

In Australia, the east and west coast humpback whale populations are listed as a Threatened species with a Least Concern status, as defined by the Environment Protection and Biodiversity Conservation Act 1999 (EPBC Act). While once Endangered, their numbers have bounced back, making them a conservation success story.

PENGUINS

ENDANGERED SPECIES AREA

There are 18 species of penguins and all are restricted to the Southern Hemisphere, with most on the Antarctic coasts and subantarctic islands.

Penguins feed on small fish and krill, catching these one at a time. They are also food themselves, for animals such as killer whales and leopard seals. On land, carnivorous birds steal their eggs and chicks.

EMPEROR PENGUIN

STATUS: Near Threatened

ABOUT: The emperor penguin is the largest of the 18 penguin species. Adults weigh up to 40 kilograms. They thrive in freezing conditions due to adaptations such as body fat, small extremities, recycling their own heat and by huddling together in large groups. They breed in colonies ranging from a few hundred penguins, to over 20,000 pairs.

NUMBERS: 595,000

FUN FACT: The emperor penguin is the only species that breeds during the freezing Antarctic winter. They form huddles of up to several hundred birds to shield the juveniles from temperatures that can drop as low as minus 60 degrees.

MAJOR THREATS: The emperor penguin population is currently stable, but they rely on sea ice to breed so are at risk from climate change and rising sea temperatures. Research suggests their population will drastically decline over the next 80 years, as sea ice melts.

THE ROYAL PENGUIN

STATUS: Near Threatened

ABOUT: The royal penguin has a distinct crest of yellow and black feathers. From their face down, they have white feathers, while their back is black.

NUMBERS: 1,700,000

FUN FACT: The royal penguin has no land-based predators.

MAJOR THREATS: It only breeds on the rocky island of Macquarie Island, which is considered part of Tasmania. While it is currently thriving on the island, it remains listed as Near Threatened because of its extremely limited breeding area. Any damage to Macquarie Island and the penguin's habitat, and the royal penguin numbers could decrease quickly.

LEAST CONCERN SPECIES	NEAR THREATENED SPECIES	VULNERABLE SPECIES	ENDANGERED SPECIES
King Penguin	Emperor Penguin	Humboldt Penguin	Galapagos Penguin
Adelie Penguin	Magellanic Penguins	Macaroni Penguin	African Penguin
Chinstrap Penguin	Royal Penguin	S. Rockhopper Penguin	N. Rockhopper Penguin
Gentoo Penguin		Fiordland Penguin	Erect-crested Penguin
Little Blue Penguin		Snares Penguin	Yellow-eyed Penguin

Albatross at Risk

Antarctica and the subantarctic islands are home to a wide range of seabirds, including petrels, terns, gulls, albatrosses, shearwaters, cormorants, gannets and boobies.

There are 24 species of albatross and 21 species of them occur in the Southern Hemisphere. Of the species, 19 occur in Australian waters and five breed in Australia.

Within Australian waters four areas have been listed as critical habitat for the albatrosses. Macquarie Island is listed as critical habitat for the wandering and grey-headed albatrosses.

Albatrosses have one of the lowest reproductive rates of any bird. All species of albatross lay a single egg. This fact, and the threats to their environment, put the albatrosses at risk.

THE WANDERING ALBATROSS

STATUS: Vulnerable

The wandering albatross is the largest of seabirds, with a wingspan reaching three metres. It can stay at sea up to a month in search of fish and squid, often covering in excess of 10,000 kilometres on its journey.

A pair of albatrosses will normally have one chick every two years, with the nests made in November and chick hatching in December.

Numbers have been in decline for some time. The current estimate is around 26,000.

ANTARCTIC TERN

Although listed as Least Concern, this tern is vulnerable to any change in habitat. This white or grey bird has a black cap on its head and a red bill. It feeds on small fish, fishing in groups of up to 40 other birds. They cooperate with other birds and defend their territory. It breeds at Macquarie and Heard Islands, as well as a number of islands in other territories.

FOCUS ON ALPINE HABITATS

Australia's alpine environment is small but spectacular. The mountain ranges have formed over 600 million years and are older than the European Alps and the Himalayas. The Australian Alps cover 15,000 square kilometres and include nine national parks.

Over 54 per cent of Australia's alpine area is in New South Wales, while the rest is in Victoria and the Australian Capital Territory. Despite the greater part of the region being in New South Wales, it still only occupies 0.54 per cent of the state. It is the smallest bioregion in New South Wales and one of the smallest in Australia.

Australia's main alpine and subalpine areas are in:

- The Snowy Mountains in New South Wales
- The Bogong High Plains in Victoria
- Central and southwestern Tasmania

Alpine area: above 1,800 to 1,850 metres

Alpine areas are found on mountains above the tree line, meaning the point where it is too cold for trees to grow. In Australia, the tree line starts about 1,800 to 1,850 metres above sea level.

Tasmania's Alpine Region

Alpine and subalpine areas occupy about 3 per cent of Tasmania's land surface, but they are rich with flora and fauna species found nowhere else in the world. Many of these are endemic.

The Snowy Mountains

Predominantly alpine and subalpine mountainous areas and tablelands, the Snowy Mountains boasts Australia's highest peak Mt Kosciuszko, which reaches a height of 2,228 metres above sea level. Kosciuszko National Park is the largest national park in New South Wales and features mountain peaks, grasslands, alpine lakes and granite boulders. Many rare or endangered plant and animal species occur within the Snowy Mountains.

There have been 34 threatened fauna species recorded in the area, including 10 mammals, 16 birds, 5 amphibians and 3 reptiles. The Australian Alps are on the National Heritage List and protected by federal law.

MT KOSCIUSZKO

PERISHER, NSW

CLIMATE CHANGE

In alpine areas a change in temperature means trees might grow at higher altitudes, which changes entire ecosystems.

The Mountain Pygmy Possum

CONSERVATION STATUS (IUCN): Critically Endangered

CONSERVATION STATUS (FEDERAL): Endangered

This small marsupial has grey brown fur on top, with lighter fur underneath and dark patches around its eyes. It feeds on Bogong moths during spring and summer, then fruits and other insects when the Bogong moths die or returns to Queensland. In winter, the mountain pygmy possum hibernates, the only marsupial that does so.

Males and females live separately, with the female occupying the best habitat areas. Breeding happens quickly in spring, with females having a litter of up to four in spring and the young being weaned about ten weeks after birth. Generally they live up to three years, although females have been known to live twelve years.

Unlike most other possums, it is mainly ground-dwelling, inhabiting alpine and subalpine boulderfields in south-eastern Australia. There are approximately 2,600 mountain pygmy possums left, living in only three known populations: Mount Higginbotham and Mount Buller in Victoria, and Kosciuszko National Park in New South Wales.

FUN FACT
The Mountain Pygmy Possum is the only Australian mammal adapted to live exclusively in the alpine zone.

MAJOR THREATS TO THE MOUNTAIN PYGMY POSSUM:

- Degradation, fragmentation and loss of habitat due to ski resort developments
- Climate change impacts this species by bringing them out of hibernation before their main food source, the Bogong moth arrives
- Predators such as foxes and cats

WHAT CAN YOU DO?

Antarctica might seem too far away to help, but your day-to-day actions can make a difference.

- Use less energy and use green energy where possible. The more sustainable your life is, the less you are contributing to climate change.
- Cut back on chemical use. Household, garden and agricultural chemicals end up in our river systems and ultimately the ocean.
- Never litter. Pick up any rubbish you see on the beach.
- Cut back on plastic use, including plastic bags, straws and balloons.
- Recycle. The less that is made and consumed, the less CO_2 emissions are impacting the environment.

SOME ORGANISATIONS THAT PROVIDE MORE INFORMATION:

Australia Antarctic Division
http://www.antarctica.gov.au

Australian Wildlife Conservancy
http://www.australianwildlife.org

The Foundation for Australia's Most Endangered Species (FAME)
https://www.fame.org.au/projects

WWF Australia
http://www.wwf.org.au

JOIN THE CELEBRATION

Australia celebrates National Threatened Species Day annually on 7 September.

FIND OUT MORE

SEARCH KEY WORDS

extinct, endangered, threatened species, vulnerable species, habitats, conservation, ecosystem, sustainability, biodiversity, Antarctic, subantarctic, Heard Island, McDonald Islands, Macquarie Island

SOURCES:

http://www.environment.gov.au
http://www.antarctica.gov.au
http://www.iucnredlist.org
http://www.australianwildlife.org

Glossary

critical: at a turning point for survival
ecosystem: the living and non-living parts of an area and the interactions between them
endangered: may soon become extinct
endemic: only found in a certain place
extinct: no longer in existence
feral predators: non-native animals that kill and eat other animals
habitat: place where plans and animals live
recovery plan: a plan for the conservation of a species
species: one kind of living thing
threat: anything that may reduce the numbers of a species
threatened: endangered or vulnerable
vulnerable: may soon become endangered

Index